# Aha Grammar

# 3

Happy House

# CoNTeNTs

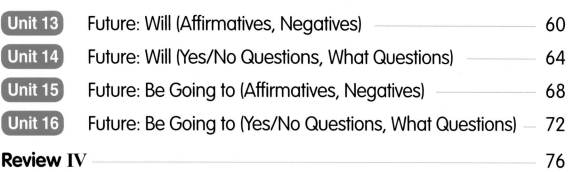

# HOW TO USE

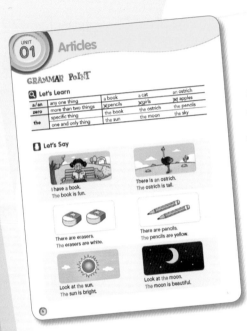

## ➜ Grammar Point

This section introduces basic grammar concepts with simple grammar charts in each unit. It also provides clear examples of how the target grammar rules are used along with illustrations.

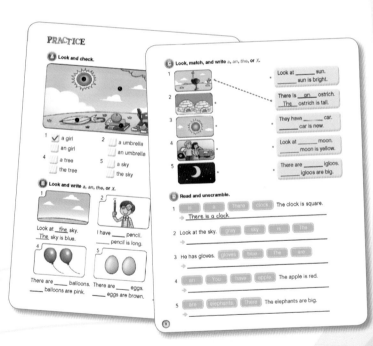

## Practice ⬅

This section provides various types of activities that allow learners to take a step-by-step approach to using the grammar rules. Learners can practice and learn the accurate use of grammar rules.

# THIS BOOK

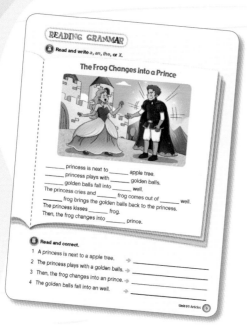

## → Reading Grammar

This section provides reading passages such as emails, journals, letters, and stories that help learners apply grammar rules in context and consolidate what they have studied. It also makes studying English grammar fun for learners.

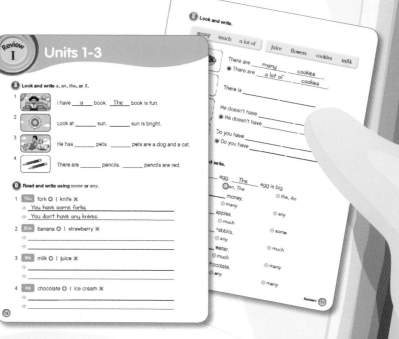

## Review ←

This section is found at the end of every chapter. It is designed to integrate grammar points that learners have studied from each unit. It can also assess and evaluate learners' understanding of the material.

# GRAMMAR POINT

## 🔍 Let's Learn

| a / an | any one thing | a book | a cat | an ostrich |
|---|---|---|---|---|
| zero | more than two things | ✗ pencils | ✗ girls | ✗ apples |
| the | specific thing | the book | the ostrich | the pencils |
| | one and only thing | the sun | the moon | the sky |

## 🎙 Let's Say

I have a book.
The book is fun.

There is an ostrich.
The ostrich is tall.

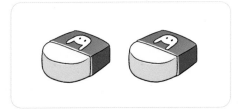

There are erasers.
The erasers are white.

There are pencils.
The pencils are yellow.

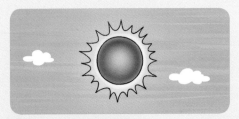

Look at the sun.
The sun is bright.

Look at the moon.
The moon is beautiful.

# PRACTICE

**A** Look and check.

1 ✓ a girl
   ☐ an girl

2 ☐ a umbrella
   ☐ an umbrella

3 ☐ a sun
   ☐ the sun

4 ☐ a tree
   ☐ the tree

5 ☐ a sky
   ☐ the sky

6 ☐ a book
   ☐ books

**B** Look and write *a*, *an*, *the*, or *X*.

1

Look at _the_ sky.
_The_ sky is blue.

2

I have _____ pencil.
_____ pencil is long.

3

She has _____ apple.
_____ apple is red.

4

There are _____ balloons.
_____ balloons are pink.

5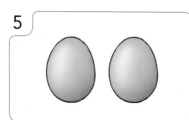

There are _____ eggs.
_____ eggs are brown.

6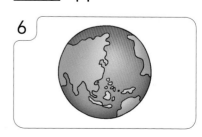

Look at _____ Earth.
_____ Earth is round.

**C** Look, match, and write *a*, *an*, *the*, or *X*.

1  
Look at _____ sun.  
_____ sun is bright.

2  
There is __an__ ostrich.  
__The__ ostrich is tall.

3  
They have _____ car.  
_____ car is new.

4  
Look at _____ moon.  
_____ moon is yellow.

5  
There are _____ igloos.  
_____ igloos are big.

**D** Read and unscramble.

1  [ is ]  [ a ]  [ There ]  [ clock. ]  The clock is square.

→ _There is a clock._

2  Look at the sky.  [ gray. ]  [ sky ]  [ is ]  [ The ]

→ _____

3  He has gloves.  [ gloves ]  [ blue. ]  [ The ]  [ are ]

→ _____

4  [ an ]  [ You ]  [ have ]  [ apple. ]  The apple is red.

→ _____

5  [ are ]  [ elephants. ]  [ There ]  The elephants are big.

→ _____

## READING GRAMMAR

**A** **Read and write *a*, *an*, *the*, or X.**

### The Frog Changes into a Prince

_______ princess is next to _______ apple tree.
_______ princess plays with _______ golden balls.
_______ golden balls fall into _______ well.
The princess cries and _______ frog comes out of _______ well.
_______ frog brings the golden balls back to the princess.
The princess kisses _______ frog.
Then, the frog changes into _______ prince.

**B** **Read and correct.**

1 A princess is next to a apple tree. → ______________________

2 The princess plays with a golden balls. → ______________________

3 Then, the frog changes into an prince. → ______________________

4 The golden balls fall into an well. → ______________________

# Some / Any

## GRAMMAR POINT

### 🔍 Let's Learn

|  | Some / Any + Countable Noun | Some / Any + Uncountable Noun |
|---|---|---|
| Affirmative | I have some apples.<br>I have some grapes. | I have some bread.<br>I have some cheese. |
| Negative | I don't have any apples.<br>I don't have any grapes. | I don't have any bread.<br>I don't have any cheese. |
| Question | Do you have any apples?<br>Do you have any grapes? | Do you have any bread?<br>Do you have any cheese? |

### 🎙️ Let's Say

I have some apples.
I have some donuts.
I don't have any grapes.
I don't have any crackers.

Does he have any apples?

Yes, he does.

We have some bread.
We have some cheese.
We don't have any milk.
We don't have any ice cream.

Do they have any milk?

No, they don't.

# PRACTICE

A **Look and circle.**

1

I have (some) I any rulers.

2

She doesn't have some I any money.

3

There aren't some I any flowers.

4
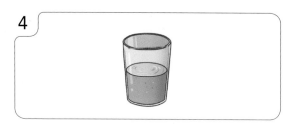
There is some I any water.

5

Do they have some I any balls?
No, they don't.

6
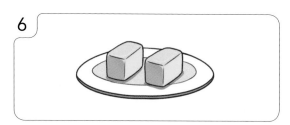
Is there some I any butter?
Yes, there is.

**B** **Read and write *some* or *any*.**

1 Do you have _____any_____ juice? Yes, I do.

2 There aren't _____ spoons on the table.

3 There isn't _____ tea in the cup.

4 He has _____ milk in the glass.

5 She has _____ books.

6 Does it have _____ bananas? No, it doesn't.

## C   Look and write *some* or *any*.

1 There is __some__ turkey.

2 There are _____ cornes.

3 There isn't _____ ham.

4 There aren't _____ candles.

5 There are _____ beans.

6 There is _____ pumpkin pie.

7 Are there _____ cranberries?
   Yes, there are.

8 Is there _____ bread?
   No, there isn't.

## D   Read and write using *some* or *any*.

1   He   sandwich ○ | donut ✕
   ➡ He has some sandwiches.
   ➡ He doesn't have any donuts.

2   You   strawberry ○ | cherry ✕
   ➡ _____
   ➡ _____

3   They   rice ○ | bread ✕
   ➡ _____
   ➡ _____

# READING GRAMMAR

**A** Read and write *some* or *any*.

## Do You Have Any Water?

**B** Read and unscramble.

1  any / Do / water? / have / you  ➡ _____

2  have / any / don't / food. / I  ➡ _____

3  I / sandwiches. / some / have  ➡ _____

4  you / any / have / Do / blankets?  ➡ _____

# Many / Much / a Lot of

## GRAMMAR POINT

### 🔍 Let's Learn

| | **Many + Countable Noun** | **Much + Uncountable Noun** |
|---|---|---|
| **Affirmative** | There are many / a lot of books.<br>There are many / a lot of pencils. | There is a lot of water.<br>There is a lot of juice. |
| **Negative** | There aren't many / a lot of books.<br>There aren't many / a lot of pencils. | There isn't much / a lot of water.<br>There isn't much / a lot of juice. |
| **Question** | Are there many / a lot of books?<br>Are there many / a lot of pencils? | Is there much / a lot of water?<br>Is there much / a lot of juice? |

### 🎙 Let's Say

There are many books.
= There are a lot of books.

There is a lot of water.

There aren't many marbles.
= There aren't a lot of marbles.

There isn't much bread.
= There isn't a lot of bread.

Are there many flowers?
= Are there a lot of flowers?

Is there much rice?
= Is there a lot of rice?

# PRACTICE

**A** Look and circle.

1  There are (many) I much I (a lot of) pencils.

2  There is  many I much I a lot of  juice.

3  There isn't  many I much I a lot of  water.

4  There aren't  many I much I a lot of  dishes.

5  Is there  many I much I a lot of  bread?

6  Are there  many I much I a lot of  cookies?

**B** Read and write *many* or *much*.

1 She doesn't have ____much____ oil.

2 There are _____ children on the playground.

3 There aren't _____ clouds in the sky.

4 He doesn't have _____ lemonade.

5 Are there _____ lions at the zoo? Yes, there are.

6 Do you have _____ water? No, I don't.

**C** Look and write.

| many much a lot of | milk egg sugar flower cheese strawberry |

1
I have ____many____ ____eggs____ .
= I have ____a lot of____ ____eggs____ .

2
He has _____ _____ .

3
You don't have _____ _____ .
= You don't have _____ _____ .

4
He doesn't have _____ _____ .
= He doesn't have _____ _____ .

5
Do you have _____ _____ ?
= Do you have _____ _____ ?

6
Does he have _____ _____ ?
= Does he have _____ _____ ?

**D** Read and write using *many* or *much*.

1 There isn't a lot of lemonade.    =  There isn't much lemonade.

2 We don't have a lot of chairs.    =  _____

3 There are a lot of trees.    =  _____

4 She doesn't have a lot of butter.  =  _____

5 Are there a lot of students?    =  _____

6 Do you have a lot of steak?    =  _____

## READING GRAMMAR

 **A** **Read and write *many* or *much*.**

### I Need Many Sandwiches

I need _____ sandwiches for the picnic. Is there any ham?

Let me see. There is a lot of ham.

Is there any cheese?

Yes, but there isn't _____ cheese. Let's buy some.

Okay. Are there any eggs?

Yes, there are. There are _____ eggs.

How about vegetables?

There are _____ tomatoes, but there isn't _____ lettuce.

**B** **Read and correct.**

1  There isn't cheese much.  ➡  _____

2  There are much eggs.  ➡  _____

3  There isn't many lettuce.  ➡  _____

4  There are tomatoes many.  ➡  _____

**A** Look and write *a*, *an*, *the*, or *X*.

1  I have ___a___ book. ___The___ book is fun.

2  Look at _____ sun. _____ sun is bright.

3  He has _____ pets. _____ pets are a dog and a cat.

4 There are _____ pencils. _____ pencils are red.

**B** Read and write using *some* or *any*.

1 You  fork ○ | knife ✕
→ _You have some forks._
→ _You don't have any knives._

2 She  banana ○ | strawberry ✕
→ _____
→ _____

3 We  milk ○ | juice ✕
→ _____
→ _____

4 He  chocolate ○ | ice cream ✕
→ _____
→ _____

**C** Look and write.

| many | much | a lot of | | juice | flowers | cookies | milk |

1. There are ___many___ ___cookies___ .
   = There are ___a lot of___ ___cookies___ .

2. There is _____ _____ .

3. He doesn't have _____ _____ .
   = He doesn't have _____ _____ .

4. Do you have _____ _____ ?
   = Do you have _____ _____ ?

**D** Read, circle, and write.

1. He has ___an___ egg. ___The___ egg is big.
   - a a, An
   - ⓑ an, The
   - c the, An

2. I don't have _____ money.
   - a some
   - b many
   - c any

3. She has _____ apples.
   - a an
   - b much
   - c some

4. There are _____ rabbits.
   - a many
   - b any
   - c much

5. There isn't _____ water.
   - a some
   - b much
   - c many

6. There is _____ chocolate.
   - a a lot of
   - b any
   - c many

# Past Simple: Be Verbs (Affirmatives)

## GRAMMAR POINT

### 🔍 Let's Learn

| Affirmative | |
|---|---|
| **Was** | **Were** |
| I<br>He<br>She  was  happy.<br>It | We<br>You  were  happy.<br>They |

| Past | Present | Future |
|---|---|---|
| yesterday | now | tomorrow |

### 🎙 Let's Say

I was sick last night.
I'm not sick now.

We were sad yesterday.
We aren't sad now.

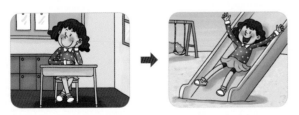

She was in the classroom this morning.
She isn't in the classroom now.

You were at the library two hours ago.
You aren't at the library now.

# PRACTICE

**A** Read and circle.

1 He (was) were a teacher before.

2 We was / were at school.

3 You was / were at work last night.

4 I was / were a dancer.

5 She was / were a cook last year.

6 They was / were rich before.

7 They was / were sick yesterday.

8 It was / were cloudy yesterday.

**B** Look and write *was* or *were*.

1  They ___were___ at the museum last weekend.

2  He _____ thirsty this afternoon.

3  You _____ at the hospital yesterday.

4  I _____ a singer last year.

5  There _____ a castle a long time ago.

6  There _____ two cars yesterday.

**C** Look and write *was* or *were*.

Last Winter

1  It ___was___ snowy.

2  They _____ in the living room.

3  She _____ happy.

4  She _____ on the ladder.

5  There _____ a Christmas tree.

6  There _____ Christmas presents.

**D** Read and write using *was* or *were*.

1  We  sad / yesterday  →  We were sad yesterday.

2  She  thirsty / three hours ago  →  _____

3  I  at the theater / yesterday  →  _____

4  You  at the park / last night  →  _____

5  It  foggy / this morning  →  _____

6  They  at home / last Sunday  →  _____

# READING GRAMMAR

**A** **Read and write** *was* **or** *were*.

## It Was My Birthday

Date: September 11, 2020

Yesterday _____ a special day.

It _____ my birthday.

I had a birthday party.

My birthday party _____ at my house.

There _____ a birthday cake.

It _____ yummy.

There _____ a lot of balloons.

They _____ colorful.

There _____ some presents.

They _____ a robot, a toy car, and a soccer ball.

I _____ very happy yesterday.

**B** **Read and unscramble.**

1 was / It / my birthday. ➔ _____

2 colorful. / were / They ➔ _____

3 There / a birthday cake. / was ➔ _____

4 presents. / were / There / some ➔ _____

# UNIT 05  Past Simple: Be Verbs (Negatives)

# GRAMMAR POINT

## 🔍 Let's Learn

| Negative | |
|---|---|
| **Wasn't** | **Weren't** |
| I<br>He<br>She    wasn't   happy.<br>It | We<br>You    weren't   happy.<br>They |

\* wasn't = was not, weren't = were not

## 🎙 Let's Say

I wasn't fine last night.
I am fine now.

We weren't happy yesterday.
We are happy now.

She wasn't on the playground this morning.
She is on the playground now.

You weren't at home two hours ago.
You are at home now.

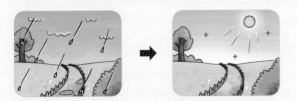

It wasn't sunny yesterday.
It is sunny now.

They weren't teachers five years ago.
They are teachers now.

# PRACTICE

## A Read and match.

+

=

1 I

2 You

3 He

4 We

5 It

6 She

7 They

was not sad.

were not sad.

You weren't sad.

I wasn't sad.

He wasn't sad.

It wasn't sad.

She wasn't sad.

We weren't sad.

They weren't sad.

## B Look and write.

1
We ___were___ ___not___ soccer players before.
= We ___weren't___ soccer players before.

2
It _____ _____ hungry this morning.
= It _____ hungry this morning.

3
You _____ _____ at home last Sunday.
= You _____ at home last Sunday.

4
He _____ _____ tall five years ago.
= He _____ tall five years ago.

**C** Look and write *wasn't* or *weren't*.

Yesterday

1 It __wasn't__ sunny.

2 They _____ in the kitchen.

3 He _____ happy.

4 There _____ toy cars.

5 There _____ a clock.

6 There _____ pictures.

**D** Read and write using *wasn't* or *weren't*.

1 They were rich before.

→ __They weren't rich before__.

2 He was at the bus stop three hours ago.

→ _____

3 It was windy this afternoon.

→ _____

4 You were at the museum last Tuesday.

→ _____

5 There were bikes by the tree yesterday.

→ _____

# READING GRAMMAR

**A** **Read and write** *wasn't* **or** *weren't*.

## My Brother Wasn't at Home

**B** **Read and correct.**

1  There weren't a scarf on the floor.  ➡ _____

2  There wasn't socks on the sofa.  ➡ _____

3  My brother weren't at home.  ➡ _____

4  My parents wasn't at home.  ➡ _____

# Past Simple: Be Verbs (Yes/No Questions)

# GRAMMAR POINT

## 🔍 Let's Learn

| Question | Answer | |
|---|---|---|
| Was I happy? | Yes, you were. | No, you weren't. |
| Were you happy? | Yes, I was. | No, I wasn't. |
| Was he happy? | Yes, he was. | No, he wasn't. |
| Was she happy? | Yes, she was. | No, she wasn't. |
| Was it happy? | Yes, it was. | No, it wasn't. |
| Were we happy? | Yes, you were. | No, you weren't. |
| Were you happy? | Yes, we were. | No, we weren't. |
| Were they happy? | Yes, they were. | No, they weren't. |

##  Let's Say

Was he hungry last night?
Yes, he was.    No, he wasn't.

Were you happy yesterday?
Yes, I was.    No, I wasn't.

Was she sick yesterday?
Yes, she was.    No, she wasn't.

Were they at the park last Sunday?
Yes, they were.    No, they weren't.

Was it cloudy yesterday?
Yes, it was.    No, it wasn't.

Were you at the beach last weekend?
Yes, we were.    No, we weren't.

# PRACTICE

**A** Read and circle.

1  Was I (Were) you at the park?    2  Was I Were  she happy yesterday?

3  Was I Were  they at the library?   4  Was I Were  it snowy last night?

5  Was I Were  he hungry last night?  6  Was I Were  they rich before?

7  Was I Were  there a bird?        8  Was I Were  there bananas here?

**B** Look, write, and check.

1  ____Was____ he angry this afternoon?

   ✓ Yes, he was.        ☐ No, he wasn't.

2  _____ they at home yesterday?

   ☐ Yes, they were.     ☐ No, they weren't.

3  _____ it windy this morning?

   ☐ Yes, it was.        ☐ No, it wasn't.

4  _____ you a firefighter five years ago?

   ☐ Yes, I was.         ☐ No, I wasn't.

5  _____ there any cups on the table?

   ☐ Yes, there were.    ☐ No, there weren't.

6  _____ there any soup in the bowl?

   ☐ Yes, there was.     ☐ No, there wasn't.

**C** **Look and write.**

Last Monday

1 ___Was___ it sunny?            Yes, ___it___ ___was___.

2 _____ they on the playground?   No, _____ _____.

3 _____ he thirsty?          No, _____ _____.

4 _____ she sleepy?         Yes, _____ _____.

5 _____ there a blackboard?    Yes, _____ _____.

6 _____ there balls?        No, _____ _____.

**D** **Read and write using _was_ or _were_.**

1 [they] hungry / last night

  ➡ _Were they hungry last night?_    Yes, ___they___ ___were___.

2 [she] a student / two years ago

  ➡ _____ No, _____ _____.

3 [it] in the garden / this morning

  ➡ _____ Yes, _____ _____.

4 [you] sad / yesterday

  ➡ _____ No, _____ _____.

# READING GRAMMAR

**A** Read and write.

## Was the Party Fun?

Hi, this is Tina.

Hi, Tina. What's up?

_____ you at the Halloween party last night?

No, _____ _____. I was sick.

_____ Tom there?

Yes, _____ _____.

Oh, I envy you.

_____ there many people?

Yes, _____ _____.

_____ there a lot of food?

No, _____ _____.
But the food was delicious.

_____ the party fun?

Yes, it _____.

**B** Read and unscramble.

1 Tom / Was / there?  ➜ _____

2 a lot of / there / Was / food?  ➜ _____

3 there / people? / Were / many  ➜ _____

4 fun? / Was / the / party  ➜ _____

# Past Simple: Be Verbs (Wh- Questions)

## GRAMMAR POINT

### 🔍 Let's Learn

| | Question | Answer |
|---|---|---|
| **Who** | Who was he?<br>Who was she?<br>Who were they? | He was Michael.<br>She was Kelly.<br>They were John and Lisa. |
| **What** | What was it?<br>What were they? | It was a ball.<br>They were puppies. |

### 🎤 Let's Say

Who was he?
He was Michael.

What was it?
It was a rabbit.

Who was she?
She was Kelly.

What was it?
It was a cat.

Who were they?
They were John and Lisa.

What were they?
They were squirrels.

# PRACTICE

**A** **Read and circle.**

1 (Who was) | What was  she?
   She was Jane.

2 Who was | What was  it?
   It was a tiger.

3 Who was | What was  he?
   He was Jim.

4 Who were | What were  they?
   They were sharks.

5 Who were | What were  they?
   They were horses.

6 Who were | What were  they?
   They were Ruth and Jeff.

**B** **Look, write, and check.**

1 ___What___ ___were___ they?

   ✓ They were bats.

   ☐ Yes, they were.

2 _____ _____ it?

   ☐ No, it wasn't.

   ☐ It was a frog.

3 _____ _____ she?

   ☐ Yes, she was.

   ☐ She was Mary.

4 _____ _____ they?

   ☐ They were my parents.

   ☐ No, they weren't.

## C Look and write.

Last Weekend

1 __Who__ __was__ he?
   He was my brother.

2 _____ _____ it?
   It was a computer.

3 _____ _____ they?
   They were my father and sister.

4 _____ _____ they?
   They were flowers.

5 _____ _____ she?
   She was my mother.

6 _____ _____ they?
   They were books.

## D Read and write.

1 __What__ __were__ __they__ ?  They were airplanes.

2 _____ _____ _____ ?  She was my grandmother.

3 _____ _____ _____ ?  He was Mark.

4 _____ _____ _____ ?  They were my teachers.

5 _____ _____ _____ ?  They were lions.

6 _____ _____ _____ ?  It was a fish.

# READING GRAMMAR

A **Read and write using *Who* or *What*.**

**What Was It?**

**B** **Read and correct.**

1 Who were they? They were birds. ➔ _____

2 What was he? He was Edward. ➔ _____

3 What it was? It was a dog. ➔ _____

4 Were who they? They were ghosts. ➔ _____

**A** Read and write *was* or *were*.

1 We ___were___ at the amusement park last Sunday.

2 It _____ cloudy this morning.

3 There _____ a lot of children at the museum.

4 They _____ sick last week.

5 I _____ at the zoo yesterday.

6 There _____ a book on the table.

**B** Look, match, and write *wasn't* or *weren't*.

1

He _____ sick yesterday.
He was fine yesterday.

2

You _____ at school last Saturday.
You were at home last Saturday.

3

It ___wasn't___ rainy this morning.
It was sunny this morning.

4

They _____ teachers five years ago.
They were students five years ago.

5

She _____ at home yesterday.
She was on the playground yesterday.

**C** **Look and write.**

1

___Was___ he hungry?
___No___, ___he___ ___wasn't___.

2

_____ you happy yesterday?
_____, _____ _____.

3

_____ they in the park?
_____, _____ _____.

4

_____ it snowy this afternoon?
_____, _____ _____.

5

_____ she sick last Monday?
_____, _____ _____.

6

_____ you at the beach?
_____, _____ _____.

**D** **Read and write.**

1 ___Who___ ___were___ ___they___ ? They were Mary and John.

2 _____ _____ _____? It was a cat.

3 _____ _____ _____? She was Jenny.

4 _____ _____ _____? They were rabbits.

5 _____ _____ _____? They were my friends.

6 _____ _____ _____? They were bees.

# Past Simple: Regular Verbs (Affirmatives)

## GRAMMAR POINT

### 🔍 Let's Learn

| Past Simple: Regular Verb | | | |
|---|---|---|---|
| **+ -ed** | play → played | walk → walked | visit → visited |
| **+ -d** | like → liked | move → moved | close → closed |
| **consonant + y → + -ied** | cry → cried | study → studied | try → tried |

| Present | | Past | |
|---|---|---|---|
| I / You / We / They | walk. | I / You / We / They | walked yesterday. |
| He / She / It | walks. | He / She / It | |

| Past | Present | Future |
|---|---|---|
| yesterday | now | tomorrow |

### 🎤 Let's Say

I washed my face this morning.

You danced on the stage yesterday.

He cleaned his room this afternoon.

She cried last night.

We played soccer last weekend.

They studied English yesterday.

# PRACTICE

**A** **Read and write.**

1 open → __opened__

2 bake → _____

3 try → _____

4 play → _____

5 smile → _____

6 cry → _____

7 visit → _____

8 wash → _____

**B** **Look and write.**

1

We ___walked___ in the park yesterday.

2

I _____ math last week.

3

You _____ TV last weekend.

4

He _____ the window this afternoon.

5

They _____ in the igloos before.

6

She _____ soup this morning.

## C Look and write.

Last Night

1 I __exercised__ .

2 My dad _____ TV.

3 My dog _____.

4 My mom _____ at my baby brother.

5 My baby brother _____.

6 My sister _____ English.

| watch | study | smile | cry | bark | ~~exercise~~ |

## D Read and write.

1 She dances at the party. → __She danced at the party.__

2 They play basketball. → _____

3 I carry my umbrella. → _____

4 He brushes his teeth. → _____

5 We visit our grandmother. → _____

6 It likes fish. → _____

**A** **Read and write.**

## My Mom Smiled at Me

Dear Katie,

How are you doing?
What did you give your mom on Mother's Day?
I _____ a gift and a card.
<u>prepare</u>

I _____ breakfast.
<u>cook</u>

I _____ the dishes.
<u>wash</u>

I _____ and _____ the house.
<u>tidy</u>          <u>clean</u>

My mom _____ at me.
<u>smile</u>

I was very happy.
Write to me soon.

Sincerely,
Mary

**B** **Read and unscramble.**

1  prepared / I / a gift and a card.    ➔ _____

2  at me. / smiled / My mom    ➔ _____

3  I / the house. / tidied and cleaned ➔ _____

4  the dishes. / I / washed    ➔ _____

# UNIT 09

# Past Simple: Irregular Verbs (Affirmatives)

## GRAMMAR POINT

### 🔍 Let's Learn

| Past Simple: Irregular Verb | | | |
|---|---|---|---|
| have ➡ had<br>sit ➡ sat<br>run ➡ ran<br>sing ➡ sang<br>drink ➡ drank | get ➡ got<br>do ➡ did<br>teach ➡ taught<br>ride ➡ rode<br>write ➡ wrote | see ➡ saw<br>make ➡ made<br>come ➡ came<br>give ➡ gave<br>eat ➡ ate | take ➡ took<br>go ➡ went<br>meet ➡ met<br>sleep ➡ slept<br>read ➡ read |

| Present | Past |
|---|---|
| I / You / We / They   run.<br>He / She / It          runs. | I / You / We / They<br>He / She / It          ran yesterday. |

### 🎙 Let's Say

I got up early this morning.

You ate sandwiches this afternoon.

He went to school yesterday.

She did her homework this evening.

We took a bus last Tuesday.

They read books last night.

# PRACTICE

**A** **Read and write.**

| saw | did | went | ~~sat~~ | bought | had | flew | swam |

1 sit → _____sat_____      2 have → _____

3 buy → _____      4 see → _____

5 do → _____      6 go → _____

7 fly → _____      8 swim → _____

**B** **Look and write.**

1
write

He _____wrote_____ a letter last night.

2
ride

I _____ a bike yesterday.

3
drink

They _____ milk this morning.

4
come

You _____ home this afternoon.

5
teach

She _____ English last year.

6
make

We _____ a snowman last winter.

## C  Look and write.

This Afternoon

1  They ___ran___ fast.　　　2  They _____ kites.

3  She _____ juice.　　4  He _____ a hamburger.

5  She _____ on the bench.　6  He _____ a bike.

| sit | eat | ~~run~~ | fly | ride | drink |

## D  Read and write.

1  You sing a song. → You sang a song. _____

2  She goes to the post office. → _____

3  They do their homework. → _____

4  He comes to my house. → _____

5  I take a shower. → _____

6  You see a movie. → _____

# READING GRAMMAR

## A  Read and write.

MAIL

| From | Martin@happyhouse.com |
| To | Edward@happyhouse.com |
| Subject | I Had a Wonderful Weekend |

Hi, Edward.

What did you do last weekend?

I _____ to the amusement park.
     go

I _____ a rollercoaster and a merry-go-round.
     ride

I _____ a hot dog and some cotton candy.
     eat

I _____ many pictures.
     take

I _____ a parade and a magic show.
     see

I _____ a wonderful weekend.
     have

I'm tired, and I should go to bed now.

Kind regards,
Martin

## B  Read and correct.

1  I goed to the amusement park.  ➡ _____

2  I haved a wonderful weekend.  ➡ _____

3  I many pictures took.  ➡ _____

4  I rided a rollercoaster.  ➡ _____

# Past Simple: Verbs (Negatives)

## GRAMMAR POINT

### 🔍 Let's Learn

| Affirmative | | Negative | |
|---|---|---|---|
| I / You / We / They<br>He / She / It | went yesterday. | I / You / We / They<br>He / She / It | didn't go yesterday. |

### 🎤 Let's Say

I didn't wash my feet this morning.
I washed my face this morning.

You didn't eat hot dogs this afternoon.
You ate sandwiches this afternoon.

He didn't clean the kitchen last Sunday.
He cleaned his room last Sunday.

She didn't do the dishes this evening.
She did her homework this evening.

We didn't study science yesterday.
We studied English yesterday.

They didn't read comic books last night.
They read books last night.

# PRACTICE

**A** Read and circle.

1 He (didn't) don't come here before.   2 I didn't / doesn't play tennis.

3 You didn't cry / cried yesterday.   4 We didn't took / take a train.

5 She didn't / doesn't dance last night.   6 You doesn't / didn't get up early.

7 I didn't ate / eat breakfast yesterday.   8 It didn't liked / like bananas.

**B** Look and write.

We ___didn't___ ___bake___ bread last Friday.
We ___baked___ cookies last Friday.

She _____ _____ her uncle last weekend.
She _____ her grandmother last weekend.

I _____ _____ my books yesterday.
I _____ my toys yesterday.

They _____ _____ Kelly this afternoon.
They _____ Brian this afternoon.

He _____ _____ presents to her yesterday.
He _____ flowers to her yesterday.

We _____ _____ an alligator last Sunday.
We _____ an elephant last Sunday.

**C** Look and write.

Yesterday Afternoon

1  They __didn't__ __sit__ on the bench.
                   sit

2  He _____ _____ a seesaw.
                ride

3  She _____ _____ ice cream.
           eat

4  He _____ _____ balls.
               have

5  They _____ _____ baseball.
          play

6  It _____ _____.
          bark

**D** Read and write.

1  You did your homework.    → You didn't do your homework.

2  We made a sandcastle.    → _____

3  I slept all day yesterday.    → _____

4  He washed his car last Sunday. → _____

5  I opened the window last night. → _____

6  She brushed her hair.    → _____

**A** Read and write.

# Today Was a Bad Day

Date: May 27, 2030

Today was a bad day.

I didn't hear my alarm.

I _____ _____ up early.  I was in a hurry.

I _____ _____ my hair.

I _____ _____ breakfast.

I _____ _____ my purse.

I _____ _____ the bus.  I ran to school.

I _____ _____ any friends.

I felt strange.  The school gate was closed.

I checked my watch.  It was Saturday.

I went back home and slept again.

| eat | bring | meet | get | take | wash |

---

**B** Read and unscramble.

1  take / I / didn't / the bus.  →  _____

2  didn't / my purse. / bring / I  →  _____

3  I / eat / breakfast. / didn't  →  _____

4  my hair. / didn't / I / wash  →  _____

# Past Simple: Verbs (Yes/No Questions)

## GRAMMAR POINT

### 🔍 Let's Learn

| Question | | | Answer | | | | | | |
|---|---|---|---|---|---|---|---|---|---|
| Did | I<br>you<br>he<br>she<br>it | drink water yesterday? | Yes, | you<br>I<br>he<br>she<br>it | did. | No, | you<br>I<br>he<br>she<br>it | didn't. |
| Did | we<br>you<br>they | drink water yesterday? | Yes, | you<br>we<br>they | did. | No, | you<br>we<br>they | didn't. |

### 🎙 Let's Say

Did you play the piano yesterday?
Yes, I did.

Did he sing this afternoon?
No, he didn't.

Did you wash the car?
No, we didn't.

Did they sit on the bench?
Yes, they did.

# PRACTICE

**A** **Read and circle.**

1  Do I (Did) you go to the park?
   Yes, we did.

2  Did I  run I ran  this morning?
   No, you didn't.

3  Does I Did  he do his homework?
   No, he didn't.

4  Did they  close I closed  the door?
   Yes, they did.

5  Does I Did  she play the violin?
   Yes, she did.

6  Did it  rain I rained  yesterday?
   No, it didn't.

**B** **Look and write.**

1
   make

   ___Did___ they ___make___ a snowman?
   ___No___ , ___they___ ___didn't___ .

2
   watch

   _____ you _____ a movie last weekend?
   _____ , _____ _____ .

3
   ride

   _____ he _____ a bike this afternoon?
   _____ , _____ _____ .

4
   paint

   _____ she _____ a picture yesterday?
   _____ , _____ _____ .

5
   sleep

   _____ it _____ this morning?
   _____ , _____ _____ .

6  
   study

   _____ you _____ English?
   _____ , _____ _____ .

**C** Look and write.

Last Tuesday

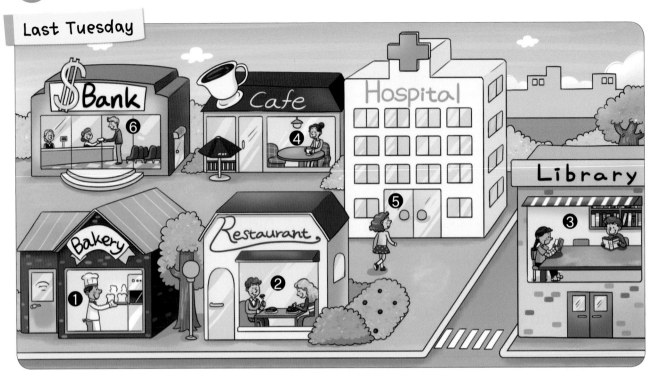

1 ___Did___ he bake any bread?
Yes, ___he___ ___did___.

2 _____ they eat spaghetti?
No, _____ _____.

3 _____ they read books?
Yes, _____ _____.

4 _____ she drink water?
No, _____ _____.

5 _____ she go to the hospital?
Yes, _____ _____.

6 _____ he give flowers to her?
No, _____ _____.

**D** Read and write.

1 They went to the library. → ___Did they go to the library?___

2 He climbed a mountain. → _____

3 It cried last night. → _____

4 She liked the present. → _____

5 You taught English last year. → _____

6 We wrote a card to our parents. → _____

# READING GRAMMAR

### A Read and write.

**Did You Read Books?**

_____ you read books today?

Yes, _____ _____. I read comic books.

_____ your brother study English?

Yes, _____ _____. He saw English cartoon movie.

How are you?

_____ your sister clean her room?

Yes, she did. She put things in the closet.

_____ you make any special food for us?

No, I didn't.

### B Read and correct.

1 Did you readed books?              → _____

2 Did your brother studies English?  → _____

3 No, I did.                         → _____

4 Did you made any special food for us? → _____

# Past Simple: Verbs (What Questions)

## GRAMMAR POINT

### 🔍 Let's Learn

| Question | Answer |
|---|---|
| What did I / you / he / she / it do yesterday? | You washed your dog yesterday.<br>I did my homework yesterday.<br>He studied math yesterday.<br>She went to the park yesterday.<br>It chased a butterfly yesterday. |
| What did we / you / they do yesterday? | You rode a horse yesterday.<br>We played soccer yesterday.<br>They flew kites yesterday. |

### 🎤 Let's Say

What did you do yesterday?
I went to school yesterday.

What did she do yesterday?
She had a birthday party yesterday.

What did you do this afternoon?
We played soccer this afternoon.

What did they do last weekend?
They flew kites last weekend.

# PRACTICE

**A** **Read and circle.**

1  What [ do I **did** ] they do last night?
They exercised last night.

2  What [ does I **did** ] she do yesterday?
She went to the zoo yesterday.

3  What [ **did** I do ] you do this morning?
I read a newspaper this morning.

4  What [ **did** I does ] he do last week?
He studied science last week.

5  What [ do I **did** ] you do last Sunday?
We cleaned the house last Sunday.

6  What [ does I **did** ] it do last night?
It slept last night.

**B** **Look and write.**

1  __What__ __did__ you do last night?
We __watched__ TV last night.

2  _____ _____ she do this morning?
She _____ soup this morning.

3  _____ _____ they do yesterday?
They _____ to the mountain.

4  _____ _____ he do last night?
He _____ a letter last night.

5  _____ _____ you do last weekend?
We _____ books last weekend.

6  _____ _____ she do yesterday?
She _____ her grandmother yesterday.

**C** **Look and write.**

|  | This Morning | This Afternoon |
|---|---|---|
| I | eat breakfast | ride a bike |
| My brother | drink milk | play soccer |
| My parents | read newspapers | exercise |

1  What did you do this morning?

(did / this morning? / What / you / do)

I ___ate___ breakfast this morning.

2  _____

(your brother / What / do / this morning? / did)

He _____ milk this morning.

3  _____

(this morning? / did / your parents / do / What)

They _____ newspapers this morning.

4  _____

(do / you / What / this afternoon? / did)

I _____ a bike this afternoon.

5  _____

(did / this afternoon? / do / What / your brother)

He _____ soccer this afternoon.

6  _____

(What / do / your parents / this afternoon? / did)

They _____ this afternoon.

# READING GRAMMAR

## A Read and write.

**What Did You Do After School?**

_____ _____ you do in art class today?

I _____ a picture.

_____ _____ you do in English class?

I _____ an essay.

My brother is ugly. He is short.

_____ _____ you do after school?

I _____ your T-shirt.

_____ _____ you do this evening?

I _____ cookies.

write   bake   wash   paint

## B Read and unscramble.

1  did / do / What / after school? / you  → _____

2  What / you / did / in art class? / do  → _____

3  you / this evening? / do / What / did  → _____

4  do / What / you / did / in English class? → _____

# Units 8-12

## A Read and write.

| Present | Past | Present | Past |
|---------|------|---------|------|
| visit | visited | get | |
| like | | make | |
| cry | | come | |
| walk | | have | |

## B Look and write.

1

**wash**

I ___didn't___ ___wash___ my feet.
I ___washed___ my face.

2

**eat**

You _____ _____ hot dogs.
You _____ sandwiches.

3

**do**

She _____ _____ the dishes.
She _____ her homework.

4

**clean**

He _____ _____ the yard.
He _____ his room.

5

**study**

We _____ _____ science.
We _____ English.

6

**read**

They _____ _____ comic books
They _____ books.

## C  Read and write.

| go | play | watch | sleep | have |
|----|------|-------|-------|------|

1  ___Did___ you ___play___ soccer this morning?

No, I ___didn't___.

2  _____ he _____ TV last night?

Yes, he _____.

3  _____ she _____ a birthday party yesterday?

Yes, she _____.

4  _____ they _____ to the museum last weekend?

No, they _____.

5  _____ it _____ well last night?

Yes, it _____.


## D  Read and write.

1  ___What___ ___did___ he ___do___ this morning?   b

2  _____ _____ you _____ last weekend?   ☐

3  _____ _____ she _____ yesterday?   ☐

4  _____ _____ they _____ this afternoon?   ☐

ⓐ She saw a movie yesterday.

ⓑ He ate breakfast this morning.

ⓒ I baked cookies last weekend.

ⓓ They washed their dog this afternoon.

# Future: Will (Affirmatives, Negatives)

## GRAMMAR POINT

### 🔍 Let's Learn

| Affirmative | | Negative | |
|---|---|---|---|
| I / You / We / They He / She / It | will be happy. | I / You / We / They He / She / It | won't be happy. |
| I / You / We / They He / She / It | will come. | I / You / We / They He / She / It | won't come. |

\* won't = will not

| Past | Present | Future |
|---|---|---|
| yesterday | now | tomorrow |

### 🎤 Let's Say

I am a student now.
I will be a doctor in the future.

You eat dinner.
You will eat dessert after dinner.

It is cloudy today.
It will be rainy tomorrow.

He studies history.
He will study English.

We are at home.
We won't be outside.

They take a bus.
They won't take a subway.

# PRACTICE

## A  Read and circle.

1  It (will be) will is  cloudy tomorrow.  2  She  will go I will goes  to the hospital.

3  We  will be I will were  late for school.  4  I  will clean I will cleaned  my room.

5  You  won't be I won't are  angry.  6  It  won't snow I won't snows  tomorrow.

7  He  won't be I won't was  a scientist.  8  They  won't do I won't did  the dishes.

## B  Look and write.

1
She _____will_____ _____be_____ a teacher in the future.
She _____won't_____ _____be_____ a doctor in the future.

2
We _____ _____ full.
We _____ _____ hungry.

3
He _____ _____ his car.
He _____ _____ his dog.

4
You _____ _____ the piano.
You _____ _____ the violin.

5
I _____ _____ swimming.
I _____ _____ hiking.

6
They _____ _____ a movie.
They _____ _____ TV.

**C** Look and write.

| Weather and Activities | | | | |
|---|---|---|---|---|
| Monday | Tuesday | Wednesday | Thursday | Friday |
| | | | | |
| | | | | |

1  be   It ___will___ ___be___ sunny next Monday.

   play   We ___will___ __play__ basketball. We __won't__ __play__ soccer.

2  be   It _____ _____ windy next Tuesday.

   fly   We _____ _____ kites. We _____ _____ airplanes.

3  be   It _____ _____ sunny next Wednesday.

   stay   We _____ _____ at home. We _____ _____ outside.

4  be   It _____ _____ snowy next Thursday.

   go   We _____ _____ skating. We _____ _____ fishing.

5  be   It _____ _____ warm next Friday.

   have   We _____ _____ hot chocolate. We _____ _____ cold juice.

**D** Read and write.

1  You will clean the house today.  →  You __won't__ __clean__ the house today.

2  He _____ _____ the dog.  →  He won't walk the dog.

3  It will be sunny today.  →  It _____ _____ sunny today.

4  They _____ _____ happy.  →  They won't be happy.

5  I will ride my bike tomorrow.  →  I _____ _____ my bike tomorrow.

**A**  Read and write *will* or *won't*.

## She Will Get Up Early

**Lisa's To-Do List for Tomorrow**

- ☑ get up early
- ☑ be at school on time
- ☒ study math
- ☑ ride a bike
- ☒ go to the park
- ☒ write an email
- ☑ read a book
- ☒ walk the dog
- ☑ do homework
- ☒ clean the house

Lisa wrote her to-do list for tomorrow. She checked what she will and won't do.

- She _____ get up early.
- She _____ be at school on time.
- She _____ study math.
- She _____ ride a bike.
- She _____ go to a park.
- She _____ write an email.
- She _____ read a book.
- She _____ walk the dog.
- She _____ do her homework.
- She _____ clean the house.

**B**  Read and correct.

1  She will rides a bike.  ➡  _____

2  She be will at school on time.  ➡  _____

3  She cleans won't the house.  ➡  _____

4  She won't studies math.  ➡  _____

# Future: Will (Yes/No Questions, What Questions)

## GRAMMAR POINT

### 🔍 Let's Learn

| Question | | | Answer | | | | | | |
|---|---|---|---|---|---|---|---|---|---|
| Will | I you he she it | be happy? go to the park? | Yes, | you I he she it | will. | No, | you I he she it | won't. |
| Will | we you they | be happy? go to the park? | Yes, | you we they | will. | No, | you we they | won't. |
| | What will you be in the future? What will you do tomorrow? | | I will be a doctor in the future. I will go to the beach tomorrow. | | | | | |

### 🎙 Let's Say

Will it be sunny tomorrow?
No, it won't.

Will they play baseball?
Yes, they will.

What will you be in the future?
I will be a scientist in the future.

What will he do?
He will help the old woman.

# PRACTICE

1 ( Will ) I Do you go shopping today?
Yes, I will.

2 Will it is I be snowy tomorrow?
No, it won't.

3 Will I Are they be scientists?
No, they won't.

4 Will he come I comes to the party?
Yes, he will.

5 Will I Does she do her homework?
Yes, she will.

6 Will you are I be late tonight?
No, we won't.

7 Will it rain this Saturday?
Yes, it does I will .

8 What will he do this afternoon?
He will watch I watches a movie.

**B** **Look and write.**

1 buy

____Will____ she ___buy___ bread?
___No___ , ___she___ ___won't___ .

2 run

_____ they _____?
_____ , _____ _____.

3 brush

_____ you _____ your hair?
_____ , _____ _____.

4 be

_____ it _____ sunny this afternoon?
_____ , _____ _____.

5 make

_____ _____ she do?
_____ _____ _____ cookies.

6 be

_____ _____ he be?
_____ _____ _____ a police officer.

## C  Look and write.

Future Dream

be    sing    play    teach

1  __Will__ she __be__ a teacher?
Yes, __she__ __will__ .

2  _____ she _____ math?
No, _____ _____ .

3  _____ he _____ a dancer?
No, _____ _____ .

4  _____ he _____ a song?
Yes, _____ _____ .

5  _____ _____ she _____ ?
She will be a pianist.

6  What will she do?
She _____ _____ the piano.

## D  Read and write.

1  They will ride their bikes tomorrow.
→  __Will they ride their bikes tomorrow?__

2  She will go to the zoo this weekend.
→  _____

3  We will visit our grandparents this Sunday.
→  _____

4  You will be a singer.
→  _____

# READING GRAMMAR

## A  Read and write.

**Will It Be Rainy Tomorrow?**

## B  Read and unscramble.

1  it / be / tomorrow? / Will / rainy    →  _____

2  go / Will / you / tomorrow? / camping  →  _____

3  with you? / Will / go / your dog Mark  →  _____

4  it / No, / won't.    →  _____

# Future: Be Going to (Affirmatives, Negatives)

## GRAMMAR POINT

### 🔍 Let's Learn

| Affirmative | | | Negative | | |
|---|---|---|---|---|---|
| I<br>He / She / It<br>We / You / They | am going to<br>is going to<br>are going to | be sad.<br>walk. | I<br>He / She / It<br>We / You / They | am not going to<br>is not going to<br>are not going to | be sad.<br>walk. |

| Past | Present | Future |
|---|---|---|
| yesterday | now | tomorrow |

### 🎙️ Let's Say

I am going to visit America next week.
= I'm going to visit America next week.

We are going to be thirsty.
= We're going to be thirsty.

It is going to be sunny tomorrow.
= It's going to be sunny tomorrow.

She is going to buy some bread.
= She's going to buy some bread.

She is not going to be late.
= She isn't going to be late.

They are not going to have a Christmas party.
= They aren't going to have a Christmas party.

# PRACTICE

**A** Read and circle.

1 We am going to / (are going to) see a movie tonight.

2 She isn't going to / aren't going to do her homework today.

3 I am going to / is going to make a cake tomorrow.

4 It is going to is / be hungry soon.

5 They aren't going to studies / study science next week.

6 He isn't going to write / writes an email tonight.

**B** Look and write.

1  read

He ___is going to___ ___read___ a letter.
He ___isn't going to___ ___read___ a book.

2  be

We _____ _____ fat.
We _____ _____ thin.

3  do

She _____ _____ the dishes.
She _____ _____ the laundry.

4  go

You _____ _____ to the dentist.
You _____ _____ to the library.

5  be

She _____ _____ angry.
She _____ _____ happy.

6  eat

I _____ _____ pizza.
I _____ _____ steak.

**C** Look and write.

1 She ____is going to____ ___paint___ a picture.

2 He _____ _____ a book.

3 She _____ _____ rollerblades.

4 He _____ _____ an airplane.

5 They _____ _____ baseball.

6 It _____ _____ sunny.

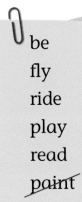

be
fly
ride
play
read
~~paint~~

**D** Read and write.

1 They are going to be doctors.

→ ___They aren't going to be doctors.___

2 I am going to meet my friends tomorrow.

→ _____

3 He is going to be angry.

→ _____

4 You are going to clean the house.

→ _____

# READING GRAMMAR

**A** **Read and write.**

## He Is Going to Be Busy Next Week

**David's Plans for Next Week**

| Mon | Tue | Wed | Thu | Fri | Sat | Sun |
|-----|-----|-----|-----|-----|-----|-----|
| pack | fly | see | ride | visit | go | come |

David is going to go on a trip to Paris next week.

He made plans for the trip.

He _____ _____ his bag on Monday.

He _____ _____ to Paris on Tuesday.

He _____ _____ the Eiffel Tower on Wednesday.

He _____ _____ on a ship on Thursday.

He _____ _____ some famous restaurants on Friday.

He _____ _____ shopping on Saturday.

He _____ _____ back home on Sunday.

He is going to be busy next week.

**B** **Read and correct.**

1   He is going to packs his bag.   → _____

2   He be going to fly to Paris.   → _____

3   He are going to ride on a ship.   → _____

4   He is going to comes back home.   → _____

# Future: Be Going to (Yes/No Questions, What Questions)

## GRAMMAR POINT

### 🔍 Let's Learn

| Question | | Answer | |
|---|---|---|---|
| Am I<br>Are you<br>Is he<br>Is she<br>Is it | going to be happy?<br>going to come? | Yes, you are.<br>Yes, I am.<br>Yes, he is.<br>Yes, she is.<br>Yes, it is. | No, you aren't.<br>No, I'm not.<br>No, he isn't.<br>No, she isn't.<br>No, it isn't. |
| Are we<br>Are you<br>Are they | going to be happy?<br>going to come? | Yes, you are.<br>Yes, we are.<br>Yes, they are. | No, you aren't.<br>No, we aren't.<br>No, they aren't. |
| What are you going to be in the future?<br>What are you going to do next week? | | I am going to be a doctor in the future.<br>I am going to visit Paris next week. | |

### 🎙️ Let's Say

Is she going to be angry?
Yes, she is.

Are they going to sleep in the house?
No, they aren't.

What is he going to be in the future?
He is going to be a firefighter in the future.

What are you going to do?
I am going to watch TV.

# PRACTICE

**A** **Read and circle.**

1 ( Is ) I Are he going to be thirsty? Yes, he is.

2 Am I Are you going to write a letter? No, I'm not.

3 Are they going to play I plays soccer tomorrow? Yes, they are.

4 Is it going to is I be windy this afternoon? No, it isn't.

5 What are you going to do I did ? I am going to read a book.

6 What is she going to is I be ? She is going to be a nurse.

**B** **Look and write.**

1 go

_Are_ you _going to_ _go_ to school?
_Yes_ , _I_ _am_ .

2 wear

_____ she _____ _____ a skirt?
_____ , _____ _____ .

3 brush

_____ they _____ _____ the dog?
_____ , _____ _____ .

4 give

_____ she _____ _____ a pen to him?
_____ , _____ _____ .

5 be

_____ he _____ _____ on time?
_____ , _____ _____ .

6 take

_____ you _____ _____ a bus?
_____ , _____ _____ .

**C** **Look and write.**

| | Saturday | | | Sunday | | |
|---|---|---|---|---|---|---|
| | visit the zoo | go fishing | watch a movie | clean the house | walk the dog | make a cake |
| **Paul** | X | O | X | O | X | X |
| **Lisa** | X | X | O | X | X | O |
| **The twins** | O | X | X | X | O | X |

1 __Is__ Paul __going to__ __go__ fishing on Saturday? Yes, he is.

2 _____ Lisa _____ _____ a movie on Saturday? Yes, she is.

3 _____ the twins _____ _____ the zoo on Saturday? Yes, they are.

4 _____ _____ Paul _____ do on Sunday?
He is going to clean the house.

5 _____ _____ Lisa _____ do on Sunday?
She is going to make a cake.

6 _____ _____ the twins _____ do on Sunday?
They are going to walk the dog.

**D** **Read and write.**

1 You are going to ride a bike.
→ __Are you going to ride a bike?__

2 I am going to play tennis tomorrow.
→ _____

3 She is going to be a cook.
→ _____

4 It is going to be rainy this Wednesday.
→ _____

# READING GRAMMAR

**A** Read and write.

## What Are You Going to Do?

| Kevin | Amy | Jim |
|---|---|---|
|  |  |  |
| sing a song | play the guitar | do a magic trick |

The kids are talking about what they are going to do for the talent show.

_____ _____ you _____ do for the talent show?

I'm going to sing a song.

_____ you _____ _____ a pop song?

Yes, I am. Amy, _____ _____ you _____ do?

I'm going to play the guitar.

That's great. _____ you _____ _____ a country song?

No, I'm not. I'm going to play a K-pop song.

_____ _____ you _____ do, Jim?

I'm going to do a magic trick.

Fantastic! _____ you _____ _____ a magic hat?

Yes, I am.

use   sing   play

**B** Read and unscramble.

1  are / going to / What / you / do?   ➡ _____

2  you / sing a pop song? / Are / going to   ➡ _____

3  going to / Are / play a country song? / you   ➡ _____

4  use a magic hat? / you / going to / Are   ➡ _____

**A** Read and write.

1  I will go fishing tomorrow.  → I __won't__ __go__ fishing tomorrow.

2  He _____ _____ his room.  → He won't clean his room.

3  We will play tennis.  → We _____ _____ tennis.

4  It _____ _____ bananas.  → It won't eat bananas.

5  They will watch TV tonight.  → They _____ _____ TV tonight.

6  You _____ _____ a subway.  → You won't take a subway.

**B** Look and write.

1
__Will__ they __brush__ their teeth?
__Yes__, __they__ __will__.

2
_____ she _____ hiking?
_____, _____ _____.

3
_____ it _____ sunny this afternoon?
_____, _____ _____.

4
_____ _____ she do?
_____ _____ _____ cookies.

5
_____ _____ he be?
_____ _____ _____ a police officer.

## C Read and write.

1 ⊗ He / ride a bike / tomorrow

→ _He isn't going to ride a bike tomorrow._

2 ◉ I / wash my hair / tonight

→ _____

3 ⊗ We / visit Paris / next week

→ _____

4 ◉ She / exercise / tonight

→ _____

5 ⊗ You / study English / tonight

→ _____

6 ◉ They / have a party / tomorrow

→ _____

## D Read and write.

1 write ___Are___ you ___going to___ ___write___ a letter tomorrow?

Yes, ___I___ ___am___ .

2 cook _____ she _____ _____ dinner tonight?

No, _____ _____.

3 go _____ they _____ _____ camping next week?

Yes, _____ _____.

4 do _____ _____ you _____ _____?

I am going to stay at home.

5 be _____ _____ he _____ _____?

He is going to be a scientist.

# Adverbs of Manner

## GRAMMAR POINT

### 🔍 Let's Learn

| Regular Adverb | | Irregular Adverb | |
|---|---|---|---|
| **+ -ly** | **-y ➡ + -ily** | | |
| slow ➡ slowly | easy ➡ easily | good ➡ well | |
| quiet ➡ quietly | happy ➡ happily | late ➡ late | |
| careful ➡ carefully | angry ➡ angrily | fast ➡ fast | |
| loud ➡ loudly | heavy ➡ heavily | early ➡ early | |

### 🎤 Let's Say

I am a careful driver.
I drive carefully.

You are a good dancer.
You dance well.

They are noisy dogs.
They bark noisily.

We are fast runners.
We run fast.

It is a slow snail.
It moves slowly.

He is a hard worker.
He works hard.

# PRACTICE

**A** **Read and write.**

1 angry → _angrily_    2 happy → _____

3 early → _____    4 quiet → _____

5 fast → _____    6 hard → _____

7 careful → _____    8 late → _____

**B** **Look and write.**

1
slow

They are ___slow___ walkers.
They walk ___slowly___.

2
loud

You are a _____ speaker.
You speak _____.

3
good

She is a _____ swimmer.
She swims _____.

4
noisy

It is a _____ bird.
It sings _____.

5
neat

I am a _____ writer.
I write _____.

6
fast

It is a _____ train.
It moves _____.

## C  Look and write.

1 He is singing ___loudly___ .
  loud

2 She is dancing _____ .
  beautiful

3 It is ringing _____ .
  noisy

4 She is talking _____ .
  quiet

5 He is reading _____ .
  careful

6 She is smiling _____ .
  happy

## D  Read and write.

1 late   He comes.          →  He comes late.

2 good   You speak English.  →  _____

3 early  We get up.          →  _____

4 sad    She is crying.      →  _____

5 poor   He is playing soccer. →  _____

6 fast   It is moving its tail. →  _____

# READING GRAMMAR

**A** Read and write.

## I Will Win This Race Easily

The rabbit said, "How can you walk so slowly?"

The turtle said _____, "Let's have a race. I can win the race."

The turtle and the rabbit had a race the next morning.

The rabbit ran _____, but the turtle walked _____.

The rabbit said, "I will win this race _____."

The rabbit took a nap and snored _____.

The turtle didn't stop and moved _____.

Finally, the turtle arrived at the finish line and won the race.

| loudly | slowly | steadily | angrily | fast | easily |

**B** Read and correct.

1 The turtle walked slow. → _____

2 The rabbit ran fastly. → _____

3 I will win this race easy. → _____

4 The rabbit snored loud. → _____

# Adverbs of Frequency I

## GRAMMAR PoINT

### 🔍 Let's Learn

| Adverb of Frequency + Verb | Be Verb + Adverb of Frequency |
|---|---|
| I always get up early.<br>You often get up early.<br>He never gets up early. | I am always late.<br>You are often late<br>He is never late. |

| Question | Answer |
|---|---|
| How often do you study English?<br>How often does he play soccer?<br>How often are you angry? | I usually study English.<br>He often plays soccer.<br>I am sometimes angry. |

### 🎤 Let's Say

|  | Mon | Tue | Wed | Thu | Fri | Sat | Sun | Percentage |
|---|---|---|---|---|---|---|---|---|
| **Always** | O | O | O | O | O | O | O | 100% |
| **Usually** | O | O | O | O | O | O | X | 90% |
| **Often** | O | O | O | O | O | X | X | 70% |
| **Sometimes** | O | O | O | X | X | X | X | 50% |
| **Never** | X | X | X | X | X | X | X | 0% |

How often do you get up early?
I always get up early.

How often are you on time?
I am always on time.

How often does he play soccer?
He often plays soccer.

How often is he a goalkeeper?
He is often a goalkeeper.

How often do they sing?
They never sing.

How often are they sick?
They are never sick.

# PRACTICE

**A** **Read and circle.**

1 It often is | (is often) hungry.

2 She never eats | eats never meat.

3 You are always | always are busy.

4 I listen usually | usually listen to music.

5 He sometimes is | is sometimes sad.

6 We always walk | walk always to school.

7 They are never | never are noisy.

8 He reads often | often reads a book.

**B** **Look and write.**

1
drink

They ___always___ ___drink___ milk.
<br>always

2
study

He _____ _____ math.
<br>usually

3
ride

She _____ _____ a bike.
<br>often

4
go

We _____ _____ to the movies.
<br>sometimes

5
be

I _____ _____ sick.
<br>never

6
be

He _____ _____ angry.
<br>often

**C** Look and write.

| | Always | Often | Sometimes | Never |
|---|---|---|---|---|
| **I** | study English | get up early | walk the dog | do the dishes |
| **My sister** | exercise | play the piano | clean her room | write a dairy |
| **My parents** | read books | go shopping | watch a movie | eat chocolate |

1 How often do you study English?

I ___always___ ___study___ English.

2 How often do you get up early?

I _____ _____ up early.

3 How often do you walk the dog?

I _____ _____ the dog.

4 How often do you do the dishes?

I _____ _____ the dishes.

5 How often does your sister exercise?

She _____ _____ .

6 How often does she play the piano?

She _____ _____ the piano.

7 How often does she clean her room?

She _____ _____ her room.

8 How often does she write a dairy?

She _____ _____ a diary.

9 How often do your parents read books?

They _____ _____ books.

10 How often do they go shopping?

They _____ _____ shopping.

11 How often do they watch a movie?

They _____ _____ a movie.

12 How often do they eat chocolate?

They _____ _____ chocolate.


**D** Read and write.

1 [usually] You are on time. → ___You are usually on time.___

2 [never] He is tired. → _____

3 [often] They play tennis. → _____

4 [always] She listens to music. → _____

**A** Read and write.

# I Always Do My Homework

I have some good habits.

I _____ _____ late for school.
<u>never / be</u>

I _____ _____ to school.
<u>usually / walk</u>

I _____ _____ my homework.
<u>always / do</u>

I _____ _____ my mom.
<u>sometimes / help</u>

My brother has some bad habits.

He _____ _____ up late.
<u>always / get</u>

He _____ _____ to school by bus.
<u>usually / go</u>

He _____ _____ computer games.
<u>often / play</u>

He _____ _____ his room.
<u>never / clean</u>

**B** Read and unscramble.

1  am / late for school. / I / never  ➡ _____

2  usually / I / to school. / walk  ➡ _____

3  late. / gets up / always / He  ➡ _____

4  cleans / never / He / his room.  ➡ _____

# UNIT 19
# Adverbs of Frequency II

## GRAMMAR POINT

### 🔍 Let's Learn

| Question | Answer |
|---|---|
| How often do you take a shower? | I take a shower every day. |
| How often does she do the laundry? | She does the laundry once a week. |
| How often does he go to the movies? | He goes to the movies twice a month. |
| How often do they brush their teeth? | They brush their teeth three times a day. |

### 🎤 Let's Say

How often do you get up early?
I get up early every day.

How often do you wash the dog?
We wash the dog once a week.

How often does he clean his room?
He cleans his room every week.

How often does he walk to school?
He walks to school twice a week.

How often do they play soccer?
They play soccer every month.

How often do they brush their teeth?
They brush their teeth three times a day.

# PRACTICE

**A** **Read and circle.**

1  I read a book (every day) / day every .

2  She goes shopping one / once a week.

3  They watch a movie every week / weeks .

4  You swim twice a week / a week twice .

5  He travels year every / every year .

6  We dance three / three times a month.

**B** **Look and write.**

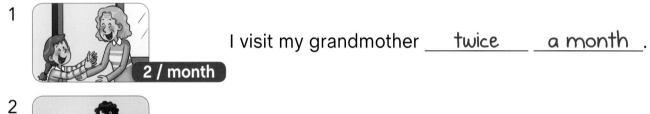

1  **2 / month**  I visit my grandmother ___twice___ ___a month___ .

2  **1 / week**  She does the laundry _____ _____.

3  **3 / year**  We go to the zoo _____ _____.

4  **every week**  You paint a picture _____ _____.

5  **every day**  He listens to music _____ _____.

6  **2 / week**  They play basketball _____ _____.

**C** **Look and write.**

| My Weekly Schedule | | | | | | | |
|---|---|---|---|---|---|---|---|
| | **Mon** | **Tue** | **Wed** | **Thu** | **Fri** | **Sat** | **Sun** |
| drink milk | ○ | ○ | ○ | ○ | ○ | ○ | ○ |
| take a school bus | ○ | ○ | ○ | ○ | ○ | X | X |
| study English | ○ | X | ○ | X | ○ | X | X |
| play soccer | X | X | X | X | X | ○ | ○ |
| eat a hamburger | X | X | X | X | X | X | ○ |
| read a book | ○ | ○ | ○ | ○ | ○ | ○ | ○ |
| watch TV | X | X | ○ | ○ | X | X | X |

1 How often do you drink milk?

I drink milk ____every____ ____day____.

2 How often do you take a school bus?

I take a school bus _____ _____.

3 How often do you study English?

I study English _____ _____.

4 How often do you play soccer?

I play soccer _____ _____.

5 How often do you eat a hamburger?

I eat a hamburger _____ _____.

6 How often do you read a book?

I read a book _____ _____.

7 How often do you watch TV?

I watch TV _____ _____.

**A** Read and write.

# I Go to the Movies Twice a Month

What did you do last weekend?

I went to the movies and met my friend.

How often do you go to the movies?

I go to the movies _____ _____.
2 / month

How often do you meet your friend?

I meet my friend _____ _____.
1 / week

What did you do last weekend, Tom?

I visited my grandmother and walked the dog.

How often do you visit your grandmother?

I visit my grandmother _____ _____.
1 / month

How often do you walk the dog?

I walk the dog _____ _____.
3 / week

**B** Read and correct.

1 I go to the movies twice months. → _____

2 I meet my friend a week once. → _____

3 I visit my grandmother a month once. → _____

4 I walk the dog three time a week. → _____

# Units 17-19

**A** Read and write.

1  He is a careful driver.  = He drives _____carefully_____.

2  She is a good swimmer.  = She swims _____.

3  They are slow walkers.  = They walk _____.

4  I am a fast runner.  = I run _____.

5  You are a loud speaker.  = You speak _____.

6  We are hard workers.  = We work _____.

**B** Read and write.

1  I am tired in the morning.

    sometimes → _I am sometimes tired in the morning._____

2  She watches TV.

    often → _____

3  They are happy.

    usually → _____

4  We eat ice cream.

    never → _____

5  He takes a bus.

    always → _____

6  You eat breakfast.

    usually → _____

**C** **Read and write.**

1 How often do you go camping?

[1 / month] I go camping ___once___ ___a month___ .

2 How often does he get up early?

[every day] He gets up early _____ _____ .

3 How often do they play the piano?

[2 / week] They play the piano _____ _____ .

4 How often does she write a letter?

[1 / week] She writes a letter _____ _____ .

5 How often do you brush your teeth?

[3 / day] I brush my teeth _____ _____ .

**D** **Read, circle, and write.**

1 You are smiling ___happily___ .

ⓐ happy          ⓑ happyly          ⓒ happily

2 He studies _____ .

ⓐ hard          ⓑ hardly          ⓒ easy

3 I _____ _____ late for school.

ⓐ often am          ⓑ am often          ⓒ often be

4 She _____ _____ a cake.

ⓐ never makes          ⓑ makes never          ⓒ make never

5 They ride bikes _____ _____ .

ⓐ a week once          ⓑ once weeks          ⓒ once a week

6 We go to the museum _____ _____ .

ⓐ twice month          ⓑ twice a month          ⓒ a twice month

# UNIT 20
# What / What Color

## GRAMMAR POINT

### 🔍 Let's Learn

| What ...? | What + Noun ...? |
|---|---|
| What is it?<br>It is a dog. | What color is it?<br>It is brown. |
| What are they?<br>They are dogs. | What color are they?<br>They are brown. |
| What do you like?<br>I like dolls. | What color do you like?<br>I like orange. |
| What does she like?<br>She likes dolls. | What color does she like?<br>She likes orange. |

### 🎤 Let's Say

What is it?
It is a cat.
What color is it?
It is gray.

What are they?
They are bears.
What color are they?
They are brown.

What do you like?
I like robots.
What color do you like?
I like blue.

What does she like?
She likes dolls.
What color does she like?
She likes yellow.

# PRACTICE

## A Read and circle.

1  Is what I **What is** it?
   It is a pencil.

2  **What color** I Color what  are they?
   They are yellow.

3  What  it is I **is it**  ?
   It is an egg.

4  What animal  **do you** I you do  like?
   I like birds.

5  What  **does she** I she does  like?
   She likes apples.

6  Sport what I **What sport**  do they like?
   They like soccer.

## B Look and write.

1
   __What__ __are__ __they__ ?
   They are shoes.
   __What__ __color__ __are__ __they__ ?
   They are blue.

2
   _____ _____ _____?
   It is a cap.
   _____ _____ _____ _____?
   It is red.

3
   _____ _____ _____ _____?
   I like teddy bears.
   _____ _____ _____ _____?
   I like pink.

4
   _____ _____ _____ _____?
   He likes balls.
   _____ _____ _____ _____ _____?
   He likes green.

## C Look and write.

1 <u>What</u> <u>does</u> <u>he</u> <u>have</u> ?  2 _____ _____ _____ _____ ?

He has a puppy.                              It is brown.

3 _____ _____ _____ ?  4 _____ _____ _____ ?

She has rabbits.                             They are white.

5 _____ _____ _____ _____ ?  6 _____ _____ _____ _____ ?

He has an iguana.                            It is green.


## D Read and write.

1 <u>What</u> <u>are</u> <u>they</u> ?                              They are socks.

2 _____ _____ _____ ?                              It is an apple.

3 _____ _____ _____ _____ ?                      They are black.

4 _____ _____ _____ _____ ?                      I like flowers.

5 _____ _____ _____ _____ _____ ?  She likes purple.

6 _____ _____ _____ _____ ?                      They have books.

# READING GRAMMAR

**A** Read and write.

**What Is It?**

**B** Read and unscramble.

1  is / it? / What  ➡ _____

2  it / What color / like? / does  ➡ _____

3  like? / do / they / What  ➡ _____

4  they? / are / What  ➡ _____

UNIT
21

# Who / Whose

## GRAMMAR POINT

### 🔍 Let's Learn

| Who ...? | Whose + Noun ...? |
|---|---|
| Who is he?<br>He is Tom. | Whose skirt is this?<br>It is Jane's skirt. |
| Who are they?<br>They are Susan and Karen. | Whose glasses are they?<br>They are Mark's glasses. |

### 🎤 Let's Say

Who are you?
I am James.

Whose hat is this?
It is Tracy's hat.

Who is she?
She is Helen.

Whose ball is it?
It is Andy's ball.

Who are they?
They are my parents.

Whose pants are they?
They are my pants.

# PRACTICE

**A** **Read and circle.**

1  Are who | **Who are** they?
   They are Lucy and Edward.

2  **Whose pen** | Pen whose is it?
   It is Peter's pen.

3  Who **he is | is he** ?
   He is John.

4  Whose **boots | boot** are they?
   They are Judy's boots.

5  Is who | **Who is** she?
   She is Molly.

6  **Whose camera** | Camera whose is it?
   It is Billy's camera.

**B** **Look and write.**

1
   __Who__ __is__ __he__ ?
   He is Bob.
   __Whose__ __toys__ __are__ __they__ ?
   They are his toys.

2
   _____ _____ _____ ?
   They are Emma and Jessica.
   _____ _____ _____ _____ ?
   They are their presents.

3
   _____ _____ _____ ?
   She is Jennifer.
   _____ _____ _____ _____ ?
   It is her bike.

4
   _____ _____ _____ ?
   We are Kevin and Alice.
   _____ _____ _____ _____ ?
   It is our dog.

## C Look and write.

1 __Who__ __is__ __she__ ?

She is Julie.

2 _____ _____ _____ ?

He is Paul.

3 _____ _____ _____ ?

They are David and Daniel.

4 _____ _____ _____ _____ ?

It is Tom's cap.

5 _____ _____ _____ _____ ?

It is Brian's ball.

6 _____ _____ _____ _____ ?

They are Nancy's rollerblades.


## D Read and write.

1 __Who__ __are__ __you__ ?                 I am Bob.

2 _____ _____ _____ ?                 She is Emily.

3 _____ _____ _____ ?                 They are John and Marry.

4 _____ _____ _____ _____ ?   It is Kelly's umbrella.

5 _____ _____ _____ _____ ?   They are Jim's shoes.

# READING GRAMMAR

## A Read and write.

### Who Are they?

___ ___ this?

It is my dad's hat.

___ ___ ___ ___ ___?

They are my sisters' mittens.

___ ___ ___ ___?

He is my dad.

___ ___ ___ ___?

They are my sisters.

## B Read and correct.

1  Who he is?              → _____

2  Whose mitten are they?  → _____

3  Are who they?           → _____

4  Whose hats is it?       → _____

# When / Where

## GRAMMAR POINT

### 🔍 Let's Learn

| When ...? | Where ...? |
|---|---|
| When is your birthday?<br>It is on April 20. | Where are you?<br>I am in the kitchen. |
| When do you go to bed?<br>I go to bed at 10 o'clock. | Where does he go?<br>He goes to school. |

### 🎙 Let's Say

When is your birthday?
It is on April 20.

Where are you?
I am in the bathroom.

When does she get up every day?
She gets up at 7 o'clock every day.

Where does he go?
He goes to school.

When do they usually go camping?
They usually go camping in September.

Where do they sit?
They sit on the bench.

# PRACTICE

**A** **Read and circle.**

1  When I (Where) does she go?
   She goes to the hospital.

2  When I Where is Christmas?
   It is on December 25.

3  When is I Is when his birthday?
   It is in July.

4  Are where I Where are they?
   They are in the classroom.

5  Is when I Where is he?
   He is in the living room.

6  Do when I When do you usually call her?
   I usually call her at night.

**B** **Look and write.**

1  _____When_____ _____is_____ Halloween?
   It is on October 31.

2  _____ _____ _____ usually hungry?
   I am usually hungry at night.

3  _____ _____ _____ wear a coat?
   She wears a coat in winter.

4  _____ _____ _____?
   They are in the library.

5  _____ _____ _____?
   She is on the playground.

6  _____ _____ _____ live?
   They live in the igloo.

**C** Look and write.

### February

| Sun | Mon | Tue | Wed | Thu | Fri | Sat |
|---|---|---|---|---|---|---|
| 1 | 2 | 3 Mother's birthday | 4 | 5 | 6 | 7 |
| 8 | 9 | 10 | 11 | 12 eat steak at Jessica's | 13 | 14 |
| 15 | 16 | 17 | 18 | 19 | 20 | 21 watch a movie at Cinema Land |
| 22 buy Tom's birthday gift at Toy World | 23 Tom's birthday | 24 | 25 | 26 | 27 | 28 |

1 ____When____ ____is____ Jason's mother's birthday?

It is on February 3.

2 _____ _____ he eat steak?

He eats steak at Jessica's restaurant.

3 _____ _____ Tom's birthday?

It is on February 23.

4 _____ _____ he buy Tom's birthday gift?

He buys it at Toy World.

5 _____ _____ _____ watch a movie?

He watches a movie on February 21.

6 _____ _____ _____ watch a movie?

He watches a movie at Cinema Land.

**D** Read and write.

1 ____When____ ____do____ you usually go to bed?   I usually go to bed at 10 o'clock.

2 _____ _____ Valentine's Day?   It is on February 14.

3 _____ _____ they?   They are in the classroom.

4 _____ _____ she come from?   She comes from Canada.

# READING GRAMMAR

**A** **Read and write.**

## When Is Christmas?

**B** **Read and unscramble.**

1 Christmas? / When / is    ➡ _____

2 you / do / live? / Where    ➡ _____

3 reindeers? / Where / your / are    ➡ _____

4 When / visit / do / my house? / you    ➡ _____

# How / How Old

## GRAMMAR PoInT

### 🔍 Let's Learn

| How ...? | How + Adjective ...? |
|---|---|
| How are you?<br>I am fine. | How old is he?<br>He is ten years old. |
| How do you go to school?<br>I go to school by bus. | How many pens does she have?<br>She has twelve pens. |

### 🎙 Let's Say

How is she?
She is sad.

How old are you?
I am eleven years old.

How do you get there?
We get there by bus.

How much bread is there?
There is a lot of bread.

How does he go to America?
He goes to America by airplane.

How many pets do you have?
I have two pets.

# PRACTICE

**A** **Read and circle.**

1 How old I (How) is he?
He is fine.

2 How much I Much how salt is there?
There is some salt.

3 How old I Old how are you?
I am ten years old.

4 How many cats there are I are there ?
There are three cats.

5 How do you I you do get there?
We get there by train.

6 Does how I How does she feel?
She feels great.

**B** **Look and write.**

1 _____How_____ ___is___ the weather?
It is sunny.

2 _____ _____ she?
She is sick.

3 _____ _____ you get there?
I get there by bike.

4 _____ _____ milk does he have?
He has some milk.

5 _____ _____ pencils are there?
There are eleven pencils.

6 _____ _____ is he?
He is 150cm tall.

## C Look and write.

1  <u>How</u>  <u>is</u>  she?

She is angry.

2  _____  _____  juice does she have?

She has a lot of juice.

3  _____  _____  their hands?

They are dirty.

4  _____  _____  muffins does she have?

She has six muffins.

5  _____  _____  they feel?

They feel surprised.

6  _____  _____  balls are there?

There are two balls.

## D Read and write.

1  <u>How</u>  <u>old</u>  <u>are</u>  <u>you</u> ?        I am ten years old.

2  _____  _____  _____?        He is tired.

3  _____  _____  _____  _____?        She is 160cm tall.

4  _____  _____  _____ come here?        They come here by subway.

5  _____  _____  _____  _____ it have?        It has four legs.

6  _____  _____  _____  _____ there?        There is some cheese.

# READING GRAMMAR

## A  Read and write.

**How Are You?**

_____ _____ you?

I am fine.

_____ _____ storybooks do you have?

I have no storybooks. I have only comic books.

_____ _____ he?

He is sick.

_____ _____ medicine does he take?

Ha-ha-ha. He is drinking some soda.

## B  Read and correct.

1  How he is?                              →  _____

2  Much how medicine does he take?  →  _____

3  Are how you?                          →  _____

4  How many storybook do you have?  →  _____

# Why

## GRAMMAR POINT

### 🔍 Let's Learn

| Question | Answer |
|---|---|
| Why are you happy? <br> Why is he late? | I am happy because today is my birthday. <br> He is late because he missed the bus. |
| Why do they stay at home? <br> Why does she study English? | They stay at home because it is rainy. <br> She studies English because she likes it. |

### 🎙️ Let's Say

Why is she sad? <br>
She is sad because she is hungry.

Why are you thirsty? <br>
We are thirsty because we are running.

Why do you study English? <br>
We study English because we like it.

Why do they stay at home? <br>
They stay at home because it is rainy.

Why does she run to school? <br>
She runs to school because she is late.

Why does he clean his room? <br>
He cleans his room because it is dirty.

# PRACTICE

**A** Read and circle.

1 (Why) I How are you hungry?

I am hungry because I don't eat breakfast.

2 Is why I Why is she in the kitchen?

She is in the kitchen because she is cooking dinner.

3 Why I What do you buy a cake?

I buy a cake because today is my sister's birthday.

4 Does why I Why does he like her?

He likes her because she is kind.

**B** Look and write.

1 ____Why____ ____do____ they like chocolate?

They like chocolate because it is sweet.

2 _____ _____ he angry?

He is angry because his sister broke his robot.

3 _____ _____ you happy?

I am happy because I got a good grade on the test.

4 _____ _____ he listen to music?

He listens to music because he is free.

5 _____ _____ she make cookies?

She makes cookies because she likes baking.

## C Look and write.

1 __Why__ __is__ he hungry?

He is hungry because he didn't eat breakfast.

2 _____ _____ she smart?

She is smart because she reads a lot of books.

3 _____ _____ they fight?

They fight because he took her toy.

4 _____ _____ he look out the window?

He looks out the window because he wants to play soccer outside.

## D Read and write.

1 __Why__ __do__ you carry an umbrella?

I carry an umbrella because it will rain.

2 _____ _____ they dirty?

They are dirty because they played in the mud.

3 _____ _____ she late?

She is late because she got up late.

# READING GRAMMAR

**A** Read and write *Why* or *because*.

## Why Are You Late?

_____ are you late?

I am late _____ I missed the bus.

_____ did you miss the bus?

I missed the bus _____ I got up late.

I got up late _____ I stayed up late.

_____ did you get up late?

_____ did you stay up late?

I stayed up late _____ I studied.

**B** Read and unscramble.

1  are / late? / you / Why      ➔ _____

2  you / Why / did / the bus? / miss   ➔ _____

3  did / stay up / Why / you / late?   ➔ _____

4  late? / did / get up / you / Why    ➔ _____

## A Read and write.

| What | Who | Where | When | ~~How~~ | Why |
|------|-----|-------|------|---------|-----|

1 ___How___ are you today?          I am fine.

2 _____ is the hat?          It is on the wall.

3 _____ are you wet?          I am wet because it is raining.

4 _____ is that?          It is a mouse.

5 _____ are they?          They are my parents.

6 _____ is your birthday?          It is on August 8.

## B Read, write, and match.

1 __What__ color do you like?          • He has five caps.

2 _____ robot is it?          • It is Tom's robot.

3 _____ many caps does he have?          • I like red.

4 _____ much water do you have?          • They are my mittens.

5 _____ sport does she like?          • We have a lot of water.

6 _____ mittens are they?          • She likes baseball.

**C** Read, circle, and write.

1 ___Where___ is the dog?          It is in the garden.
   (When / (Where))

2 _____ books are they?          They are Jenny's books.
   (Who / Whose)

3 _____ much milk do you have?   I have some milk.
   (How / What)

4 _____ does she like?          She likes bananas.
   (How / What)

5 _____ is he late?          He is late because he missed the bus.
   (Why / How)


**D** Read, circle, and write.

1 ___Who___ is he?   He is my brother.
   (a) Who          (b) What          (c) When

2 _____ pants are these?   They are my brother's pants.
   (a) Who          (b) Who          (c) Whose

3 _____ do you go to school?   I go to school by bus.
   (a) How          (b) Who          (c) Where

4 _____ apples are there?   There are nine apples.
   (a) What          (b) How many          (c) How

5 _____ is Christmas?   It is on December 25.
   (a) When          (b) Where          (c) Why

6 _____ does she study hard?   She studies hard because she has a test.
   (a) When          (b) Why          (c) Where

7 _____ do you have?   I have pencils.
   (a) What          (b) Where          (c) Who

8 _____ does she like?   She likes pink.
   (a) Who          (b) How          (c) What color

# GRAMMAR SUMMARY

## Past Simple: Be Verbs (Affirmatives)

| Affirmative | |
|---|---|
| **Was** | **Were** |
| I / He / She / It  was  happy. | We / You / They  were  happy. |

## Past Simple: Be Verbs (Negatives)

| Negative | |
|---|---|
| **Wasn't** | **Weren't** |
| I / He / She / It  wasn't  happy. | We / You / They  weren't  happy. |

\* wasn't = was not, weren't = were not

## Past Simple: Be Verbs (Yes/No Questions)

| Question | Answer | |
|---|---|---|
| Was I happy? | Yes, you were. | No, you weren't. |
| Were you happy? | Yes, I was. | No, I wasn't. |
| Was he happy? | Yes, he was. | No, he wasn't. |
| Was she happy? | Yes, she was. | No, she wasn't. |
| Was it happy? | Yes, it was. | No, it wasn't. |
| Were we happy? | Yes, you were. | No, you weren't. |
| Were you happy? | Yes, we were. | No, we weren't. |
| Were they happy? | Yes, they were. | No, they weren't. |

## Past Simple: Regular Verbs

| Past Simple: Regular Verb | | | |
|---|---|---|---|
| **+ -ed** | play ➡ played | walk ➡ walked | visit ➡ visited |
| **+ -d** | like ➡ liked | move ➡ moved | close ➡ closed |
| **consonant + y ➡ + -ied** | cry ➡ cried | study ➡ studied | try ➡ tried |

# Past Simple: Irregular Verbs

| Past Simple: Irregular Verb | | | |
|---|---|---|---|
| have ➡ had<br>sit ➡ sat<br>run ➡ ran<br>sing ➡ sang<br>drink ➡ drank | get ➡ got<br>do ➡ did<br>teach ➡ taught<br>ride ➡ rode<br>write ➡ wrote | see ➡ saw<br>make ➡ made<br>come ➡ came<br>give ➡ gave<br>eat ➡ ate | take ➡ took<br>go ➡ went<br>meet ➡ met<br>sleep ➡ slept<br>read ➡ read |

# Past Simple: Verbs (Affirmatives, Negatives)

| Affirmative | | Negative | |
|---|---|---|---|
| I / You / We / They<br>He / She / It | went yesterday. | I / You / We / They<br>He / She / It | didn't go yesterday. |

# Past Simple: Verbs (Yes/No Questions)

| Question | | Answer | | | | | |
|---|---|---|---|---|---|---|---|
| Did | I<br>you<br>he<br>she<br>it | drink water yesterday? | Yes, | you<br>I<br>he<br>she<br>it | did. | No, | you<br>I<br>he<br>she<br>it | didn't. |
| Did | we<br>you<br>they | drink water yesterday? | Yes, | you<br>we<br>they | did. | No, | you<br>we<br>they | didn't. |

# Future: Will (Affirmatives, Negatives)

| Affirmative | | Negative | |
|---|---|---|---|
| I / You / We / They<br>He / She / It | will be happy. | I / You / We / They<br>He / She / It | won't be happy. |
| I / You / We / They<br>He / She / It | will come. | I / You / We / They<br>He / She / It | won't come. |

# Future: Will (Yes/No Questions)

| | Question | | Answer | | | | |
|---|---|---|---|---|---|---|---|
| Will | I<br>you<br>he<br>she<br>it | be happy?<br>go to the park? | Yes, | you<br>I<br>he<br>she<br>it | will. | No, | you<br>I<br>he<br>she<br>it | won't. |
| Will | we<br>you<br>they | be happy?<br>go to the park? | Yes, | you<br>we<br>they | will. | No, | you<br>we<br>they | won't. |

 # Future: Be Going to (Affirmatives, Negatives)

| Affirmative | | | Negative | | |
|---|---|---|---|---|---|
| I<br>He / She / It<br>We / You / They | am going to<br>is going to<br>are going to | be sad.<br>walk. | I<br>He / She / It<br>We / You / They | am not going to<br>is not going to<br>are not going to | be sad.<br>walk. |

 # Future: Be Going to (Yes/No Questions)

| | Question | | Answer | |
|---|---|---|---|---|
| Am<br>Are<br>Is<br>Is<br>Is | I<br>you<br>he<br>she<br>it | going to be happy?<br>going to come? | Yes, you are.<br>Yes, I am.<br>Yes, he is.<br>Yes, she is.<br>Yes, it is. | No, you aren't.<br>No, I'm not.<br>No, he isn't.<br>No, she isn't.<br>No, it isn't. |
| Are<br>Are<br>Are | we<br>you<br>they | going to be happy?<br>going to come? | Yes, you are.<br>Yes, we are.<br>Yes, they are. | No, you aren't.<br>No, we aren't.<br>No, they aren't. |